Exact Colour of Snow

BY THE SAME AUTHOR

The Last Days of Petrol
Shearsman Books, 2022

Exact Colour of Snow

Bridget Khursheed

Shearsman Books

First published in the United Kingdom in 2025 by
Shearsman Books Ltd
PO Box 4239
Swindon
SN3 9FN

Shearsman Books Ltd Registered Office
30–31 St. James Place, Mangotsfield, Bristol BS16 9JB
(this address not for correspondence)

www.shearsman.com

ISBN 978-1-84861-967-8

Copyright © Bridget Khursheed, 2025.

The right of Bridget Khursheed to be identified as the author of this work has been asserted by her in accordance with the Copyrights, Designs and Patents Act of 1988.
All rights reserved.

Acknowledgements

Some of these poems or versions of them first appeared in *Gutter, Trespass, The Eildon Tree, The Rialto, Ambit, One Hand Clapping, Obsessed with Pipework, Southlight, Iota, Valve, Causeway/Cabhsair, Poetry Scotland, Orbis, Snakeskin, Up the staircase, The Lake, Poetry Scotland Open Mouse, Message in a bottle, Monkey Kettle, Biggar Poetry Garden, Pulsar, Poetry Monthly, The Delinquent, Pure Slush, The Shop, Fire, Shadowtrain*; the sequence 'A Confinement' was runner up in the Wigtown Poetry Alastair Reid Pamphlet Prize 2022; the poem 'Talking about riding horses yesterday morning' was commended in the Bassetlaw Writers Poetry Competition.

CONTENTS

Before advertising / 11
Plants I overlook / 12
…talking about riding horses yesterday morning / 13
In the textile gallery / 14
Cowboys and cowgirls / 15
The dye chemists / 16
The little gothic orangery / 17
The exact colour of snow / 18
A confinement / 19
Orienteering outside Jedburgh / 27
The shrubbery snowdrops / 28
The fruit trees / 29
Lovers Farm / 30
Story of your friend the poet / 32
Feeding the baby / 33
Hairst / 34
News of a friend / 35
This is the weather / 36
a choice / 37
The flood / 38
Under surveillance / 39
Berwick Station at night / 40
The bridge loves the firth / 41
A chemical examination of Melrose Abbey / 42
The tanning pits / 43
Dye works / 44
Industrial lichen / 45
Leaving home / 46
Frankenstein / 47
Today / 48
Knockturne / 49
The drove road / 50
Missing the queimada / 51
Tryst at the Ménagerie / 52

Another cold war / 53
The hairsheep / 54
Kestrel / 56
Digital age / 58
Thinking about Embla outside Edinburgh / 59
The mews house / 60
Border snow / 62
Angel / 63
The bomb cats / 64
A walk around Preston Island / 65
Firing range / 66
What you were left with / 68
Collecting seaweed / 69
Doggerland harvest / 70
Auto-immunity / 71
Old Biddy / 72
Saltmarsh / 75
French room / 76
The darning flat / 78
Climbing above Kinlochleven / 79
The trouble with lichen / 80
So here we go again / 82
Rain was red at the end / 83

Notes / 85

Exact Colour of Snow

For the Bedgebury girls

Before advertising

We have these shoes in this factory:
buy them if you want
or need them.

Plants I overlook

they're not like John Clare's plants
on the rubbish heap

or where they found the iguanodon
bone in the cuckoo field

but the plants in my garden
the ones I see every day

cross those small leaves of nestle
by the dog skull moss

guide stones sunk in earth
plants now entangled in couch

grass wet with the breath of rain
I overlook these plants

because they speak our name

...talking about riding horses yesterday morning

a sunny day blackberries each seed-glove shining
not wet but early and the grass all web-pocketed
and you were telling me about the woman
who kept her dog's hair and
made it into a waistcoat and now the dog's dead
she smells and combs it, a coat too hot to use.

the bitter shit smell of the chicken battery,
dogs shooting after the farm cat,
Blackthorn's big clompy rump pigging it all summer,
the gloom of Commonside trees, I knew insanity
just as you said 'that's special'.

                                    in the green lane
we hold hands across the agitating space between us
married since forever, since our children were young
and I know you as much as I know
the hedge fruit. your smile.
fresh each year and the taste anybody's guess.
and, in spite of all the sun, you kicked off again.

In the textile gallery

Some of the substances contained in lichen
make bright dye. Brush past a lily's stamen
and your shirt is streaked with red and orange
showing against nap or strong pattern.

In Schunck's laboratory, flowers grew on desks,
grasses twisted in the many-drawered chests
and, one corner set aside, the place for cotton.
Each strand dropped in a vial specked with forgotten
leaves, stalks, shellfish, reeds and rock
that he hauled back into a finely written log.

Colours the clothmen fought to use in their design
resplendent in sitcom cover for chaise longue
and pelmet. Fabrics that still give me a pang
stretched in ranks of glass case and machine.

Cowboys and cowgirls

He paid money to marry her;
his first wife had died of

suffocation – he called it a fever.
and she was available

for a few dollars.
He refused to talk to her.

So did his son. So did the dogs.
Talking to herself, she learnt to shoot,

to whistle and play the spinet.
Finally she kills an attacker

and they admit she is the new model wife.
Sadly, three or four days later,

she drowned in the fat she used
to cook his breakfast. He was sorry

and buried her next to his first wife.

The dye chemists

Schunck and Friedländer in a railway carriage
leaving Manchester, an accident
their patrons cannot like, to share
pflaume im glas in a Bramhall villa.

A familiar tunnel's momentary darkness
smokes the window, obscuring
the viscous patina of mills
and workforce faces.

Schunck's eyes close: 'colours inside
on the cloth bales are mine,'
and he imagines the new orange;
its chemistry on a hip's thrust.

Friedländer presses his handkerchief
to the glass: its pattern of dirt
reminiscent of the arcil lichen
roccella tinctoria.

The daily train released.
Smoke evaporating, they return
to their appetites, ocular exercise
in an examination of woollen fibres,

discussing the translation of Virgil
worked on for years by a coloursman
acquaintance; its incomplete notes and song,
its binding, red calf skin.

The little gothic orangery

Best work I did there
but I had nothing to do with oranges
the glass panes the cutting of them
and their angles
we had worked on stained glass
and its leading but these
the panes their fine-ness
a meadowsweet head
cut down its shapes
in glass and the curve of it
all to hold oranges
I had nothing to do with oranges

And when we placed the glass there
the rain came in from the hills
we saw its curl
in the glass laid on hessian
in trays from the gardener
he had lent us
before the oranges which might fill them
and then each piece
its position as intricate
as a flowerhead as grass seeds
or crops a harvest of glass
cut and winnowed
with lath and putty
into a shape that caught the hills
each piece of them
their incline and steep upwards
slope in the window's pattern
I could only look out
I had nothing to do with the oranges

The exact colour of snow

Tumbled like lost bedsheets
in the garden, it lies exhausted
only blocking flowers from bloom
and birds from seed.
Running down half-hearted but thick
these greybacks linger in odd drifts.

From an upstairs window in the baby hours
the second fall was white
flat on the garden and the patio.
No expectations. That stuff
unnoticed by the sleepy peeing child.

Walking the up-way past the hill
days back, it came strong
and quiet then mint-thin,
the light quite yellow.
Snow toothpasting the lines
shapes the geometry of air.

But we've forgotten now
and it's dropped in gloopy bundles,
cushions that the wren can perch on
and it stays so long
rumpled and torn by footprints
and the thin tracks of buggies
until its last petals green.

A confinement

Last day in July dug beneath withered plants
empty soil is friable then potatoes
perfect as eggs unbroken after disaster.
I chuck them in the trug. More come, some I miss.

The house looks dark and limited from here.
Television off, computer, phone on the wall
telling, waiting to tell more. The buddleia black
in twilight winking without butterflies.

More potatoes in the ground if only I could find them.
5 lettuces, of which 3 have been eaten,
2 still in the ground; 2, perhaps 3, bags of spinach;
2 bags of radishes; some spring onions;

4 strawberries; a couple of pounds of green tomatoes
yet to ripen under a restrained sun;
plentiful herbs; and, protected by nettles and a fence,
brambles on land that isn't ours.

*

Afterwards you close your eyes and tell me
that you see only blackberries:
facets of reflected light on black.
I don't believe you

but when I try, I see them too:
great swathes of fruit better and more succulent
even than the sharp bush
we've just plucked bare.

*

Tea on a slack-backed café chair, my stomach baby-
awkward seeks a comfortable position.
You've told me this unexpected confession twice
but it's your sex life. And you are a three-month colleague.

Should I tell you I'm pregnant? Add our boss
greeted me today with a post-prandial, "Hello baby"?
I look at the exhibition prints on the wall
and thank god they're not saying anything.

*

In the uncleaned ladies, smashed hulls ooze on the wall:
hopes hatched to die. I'd watched them in the cubicle
pattered intricately and still,
imitating the grey formica with a convoluted velvet.

To another lady's eye, a thing of fear, or an easy target?

Roots on the pink that was pulled up when weeding.
A scrap and roots are ghostly through a glass jar.
Another plant out of nothing.

These moths should have flown away into highest corner
These moths stayed in the daytime box they hatched in
chameleoning their space not invulnerable but
an air we must walk every day away from our screens.

*

Every night I lose a hand or leg.
I seem to seek these dreams of amputation
like the American so in love with disability
he guillotined an arm, hid it in the freezer.
Only my dream must be about losing you:
your growth away from me.

A man on the street walking towards and past me.
I pray you smile and don't say goodbye.

*

I saw my garden again. The shape of my childhood
home stretched along the extension: the walls,
the overgrown shrubs and lawn. This was last night's dream.
An adult garden has no cedar,
no circular bloom of rhododendron
big enough to hide in, no fig;
instead the potato crop is limited
and a new wasp lays and splits the rose stems.
And all this garden is mine.

*

Pots of dull earth lined up waiting here and doing nothing. Why were they planted? The daily walk and look are an unrewarded chore. Seed trays cramped and tight offer a more fertile glance. Black earth on the windowsill is vital and waiting shows a tiny green. Domestic cultivation is safer, kinder than life in the coldframe cast in tombola; yet half of all these plants die later from holiday drought.

*

Nine months with you on a desert island.
And I want a pint of cider.

*

It is the aftermath that brings me back.
The empty meadow and river and sky revealed
knife-sharp after the site's historic absence,
while behind me the walls leap up to hide

a welling anger. A space not mine to fill,
beyond the bricked-up door low in the footpath wall.
Rooms I was never inside, an invisible tide
that cuts me down through the very stone points.

*

Lost in the pram shop unknown and expensive territory
where we aim our gaze carefully and not at salespeople.
If only I could read the labels, it would be comprehensible,
part of my general delusion: all this is something to be passed.

You can have a baby, like a good job, after ante-natal classes.
But here we are alone, with the women with cold-plated eyes:
intelligence can't win against committed purchase
unless we scarper pretty fast-ish.

*

Radishes left too long do not produce bigger roots. Leaves, ragged and with a dull sheen, shoot hopefully to seed. They should have been thinned months ago. No more harvest; just a row battling the nettles and the spinach. The tomato plants are in the cold frame. Dug into the black earth of its base from which a nettle prematurely springs. In three months since the ground was cleared, no other weed has appeared inside. Today a thunderstorm watered the tomatoes. The cold frame can kill in hot weather. Plants inside – lupins, lobelia seedlings, all in one seed tray, sunflowers, tomatoes – wilted in its plastic confines. Like a dog in a car, there's no way out. The crack of air does little without watering. Okra in the black pots, lettuce in orange and black but outside, orange cucumber. Is it too late? The seed packets are taut and inscrutable. Runner beans planted three weeks ago outside and according to the packet, have yet to show green. The Spinach Sigma Emerald alone is a success and harvested repeatedly. The seeds were two years old. Nettle and dandelion grow most freely although they have yet to encroach the plot except the former amongst the strawberries. And lupins and lobelia wait for planting on outside. Lettuce and extra tomato plants are dug in already cottage style through the flowers. They waited since early May. All the seed trays and pots on the patio, house plants, and the newly bought, wait for the gardener's next watering and planting.

*

My old ways are lost with your banging on the roof.
And I can't lie on my tummy anymore.
Your decorous rustle, scheduled, is now rushing loud;
swelling out from me like a baboon on a tree.

*

Stretch out your fronds and yellow flowers
and give me cucumbers when I walk outside.
Touch my lips, strawberries,
and potatoes, pop from the soil.

Instead yesterday's lettuces shuffle amongst the rockroses,
green tomatoes hard-balled hide from the sun
and slugs eat cucumber leaves.
Weather is sticky enough to glue even my own legs together.

*

The cold frame newly-built turns blue-stained.
A job so occupying approaching rain goes unseen.
A half a minute, minutes, ten all allow a little more
fragile drying time. Thick drops well

into cracks now covered with an old groundsheet
and rapidly less and less paint.
Lupin flowers ranked on the terracotta tiles.
No flowers this year but, grown strong,

they ache to escape small pots.
Last year, this group would be in the ground.
And slugtoppled. Leaving them
root-taut is accidentally the right decision.

*

I rush back from my London meeting to recall
your transparent perfection. .8mm out.
Your kidney – of which, I keep reminding myself,
you have two – may be fine or may never function.
All reassure me. In the ultrasound anteroom,
other couples spoon as if at a teenage disco.
All that unbearable waiting.
.8mm on a kidney but now you are perfect.
Kicking with your cousin's calves
getting in the clinician's way
perhaps on purpose. I feel like glorious rampage
but instead close this door with a small click.

*

Tearing feather after feather from a small prey,
a sparrowhawk plucks outs ten extravagant minutes.
Birds flutter in the holly tree wanting their own food
until the raptor takes it unadorned mouthful.

*

The mood of leafy places empty churches
mould mildew breath of damp enclosed air.
decayed flowers mouldering wainscot
old bread and Herzog's rat.

*

A nurse waters the one plant on the windowsill.
"Nobody does it but me," she says. It's her shift end.
The radio's on but drowned by my baby's heartbeat.
I jab a button each time I feel its movement.
"Don't you move," she said. Ten fifteen twenty minutes ago.

Blood pressure goes down as well as up.
This time I get out. A lift home with the lights
hammering the bowl of the town.

*

Each in small padded cells within earshot
every five minutes lasting a minute
until taken downstairs. Unfinished blanket.
In the corner of the long studio
white with sun lie overlooked tinsel
toys made by children last year.
The empty floor stretches away from them.
Fear of the unformed, yellow light on a face
and in the station an odd greenwhite
shine on a man's ear; Faisal's bright eyes
closed but open; in the hospital light
they're hazel; dark brown in day.

*

Small complete people.
My baby boy, milk drunk and mimicking
a fish, flops in his newborn glass bowl.
This is penthouse maternity.
The main hospital shows white, surrounded
by the small figures of the authentic sick,
then shadowed. A cloud line that runs to the hills
beyond and lifts. I remember that green,
those walking years, and see those to come
through my window. I look at my son.
I look at my son.
I look at my son again.

*

The fox walked back past the kitchen window
on its way home through my rockery.
I was doing the washing up
when its head appeared by the pots and honey plant

under the clothesline to be driven off by the cat.
I've seen the fox a few times since then.
Its redness, paler than expected,
pops into view again in my imagination.

Washing or preparing my son's food,
quickly my eyes jump up to see it appear.
It doesn't. Although its smell still lingers by the shed,
I'm forgetting its light tracks.

Orienteering outside Jedburgh

Wildcat cleuch is still full of snow
but each virtual contour
is marked with a bunting
like a row of faded flags

announcing it is warm here.
These birds have come from Norway
to tease out mountain atoms, kernels
and midge crumbs.

Why they stopped in Lanton
is anybody's guess? The wind?
Or magnets?
Oh they look so good –

the geologists of snow
where the science was invented.
In theory, the whole
hill is now woody and tame

but then each snow flake
bunting flocks
anti-cycling back into their weather
blue sky arctic home.

The shrubbery snowdrops

Under the rhododendrons, they peer into a spring
in cloudy cataracts.
Ladies walking the little path
through the fernery
said the same thing.

It was better in our day.
The long prospect to an urn,
a classical joke,
we were all wits;
now obscured in twilight
thrilling only to the midday sun.

The draped velvet and crush of chairs
and tapered tables tipping to the swing
of bell-like skirts:
can flowers remember?

They have spread and spread.
The recovered path is snow and stones.

The fruit trees

1.
The espalier outgrown
arthritic on the southern aspect's brick.
A kind of devilment
its limbs jointed like a cripple's
elbows and twisted
thick and not by wind
but the old gardener's careful pruning.
One golden sun high in its thicket
touched by the first frost
and the blackbird in its nesting twigs;
the bird's eye another small fruit.
Uncollected untended
these trees fret the garden wall
barren without design.

2.
That apple against my wall
an outstretched hand with golden rings
guarded by blackbirds
to grasp a hundred years.

It has grown hirsute
parasitic with bluetits and wren
who twist and swarm to feast
through lichen and insect.

A pauper's banquet
offered by a rich man,
thick with life, succouring,
about to die.

Lovers Farm
For The Reverend A E T Hobbs

The farm's over. Background to an old man's walk,
it reeks of schemes and diversification wheezes.
His familiar path rutting through outbuildings extracted
like teeth to accommodate planning permission;
loose change, a child's game, dug into the barn's flinty edge.

He doesn't lament cows nosing stalls.
Instead marks the new rise of the landscaped horse-pond
with a white stone quietly submerged
and confused with fallen leaves;
plants his own bulrushes with a vigorous illegal shake
then circuits Greenlands down to The Wish.
Averil alone remembers boy and dog careering in a cornfield.
She tied them up in a poem but he still ignores her call.

There are seven oaks to the churchyard
as he treads round past the private fishing.
He bears witness to each.
The hitchhiker – see a branch like an uplifted thumb.
The lips – bark scarred and still swollen like a boxer's.
The horseshoe – an anonymous plough-hand's work
but restored with his own nails and hammer.
The trees tell on. To anyone watching
he moves so slowly with the fat dog at his tail,
he could be the last of them.

A group of houses turn their back on Firle Beacon
as he walks up to the church.
Intermittent wallflowers spattering the mud.
A lone man had last year's fishing for the season;
and probably will again. No one else walks.
Sometimes unseen a girl rides her horse
destroying delicate seedlings in the dusk.

Averil and her sisters, the farm's dead owners,
wait for the livestock to come home.

Story of your friend the poet

She dressed like normal people.
You inhale slowly, your baker's hands
approving that night we hung around
the pool bar on X Street.
They wouldn't let us in.
I made you drive me home drunk.

Were you a breadmaker
before or after I met you first?
Hair on your lip, stance awkward
– someone about to hit,
they had done –
trousers slack and that old t-shirt.
Big truck.
            Knowing
my habit of little labels
without even seeing my flat
and filing cabinet.
Oh the end of your bed
and the bad excuse later.

I remember you America,
your name began with T.
You came loaf in hand.
You wouldn't recognise me now.

Feeding the baby

A self-confessed breasts man:
you weren't put off by mine,
anticipating their childbirth ballooning,
the rock-hard arrival of the milk
and all the lush tenderness of feeding.

But days with me on the sofa
trapped by a hungry mouth
while you fed me
sandwiches or meals as appropriate,
the dull suck and posset,
the lumpen rocket of lopsided breastdom,
change your mind.

Drawing your own conclusions, you remark
that now you can view my breasts
easily, they've become flesh
representatives of familiar domestic things
like the kettle, you pause, or like the bread bin.

Hairst

The hedge, plashed but unlaid, makes a fist of early autumn hawthorn:
elder with tight berries and a bright fruiting rowan,
cans and a twist of paper or supple plastic tied up in damp beaten grass.
The Kelvin below I think:

its waters reveal in glimpses; tease with flicks of absent
otters and dippers. Meanwhile we stitch our way to Tesco's
the big one by the tower blocks,
to buy a swimming costume. This tarmac path playing field edge

is maximum bird. Warblers. You picked the route;
tell me you thought I would like it.
Beyond the hedge and river, I suddenly see all the open fields of Maryhill.
Strike the harvest. Come home.

News of a friend

The salt museum is closed
its quiet yard and expositions
surrounded by saltmarsh
the uneven car park
the only child's entertainment
fields of water and their channels
inaccessible across a culvert
promising an explanation
metal pipes and drainage
it is almost clear
how the sun burns away the sea
and the salt appears
an ancient method of reduction

your death four years on
a door one cannot get through
a distillation not noted
because life kept us busy
the industrial lagoon tended
valves open under sun
and amongst martins
the protection of loose overalls
soaked by sweat, visors,
concentration on process
raking the personal mine.

This is the weather

Breaking the ice path to the back door with a shovel
the blows must be repeated and prodded and hard

the ice lies shattered and I kick it for minutes
then go inside. Later there is a perfect blue sky

all the trees have a light that glows
and the crows and bluetits put the ice back together

a choice

face in the gun cupboard
flags uneven to my sole
it's the time of spiders
and webs haze the room's
cracks of air

there's rabbits to be collected
that fence between us and Stocks
all the apples rolling down the hill
and she's singing
clattering the range

so close in the tight old house
she'll stop when I go

The flood

There's been nothing like this
since you died, the stream
oozes finer than water
and the air is a distillation.

Why does that cherry tree hurt?
It's washed over with blossom
engulfed in a tide
that's ripped branches open

buds drip out blooming
into petals of rosy blood
and the water of the stream
ready at the roots

washes each flower away.

Under surveillance

The shadow creeps up the wall opposite.
I'm half asleep, feeding the baby,
not sure if I believe my eyes.
The neighbour leaves for her early cleaning job:
lights off and the frame of her front door
tight shut again; the pattern of her curtain gone.
She doesn't look up.

My son uses the shadows of the window frame
as truck routes and train tracks.
Every now and then they disappear.

Like every day, Faisal plane-spots outside, stopping
to scan the skies, plane he says in an unknown language.
Mostly it's above cloud out of sight
but sometimes a training flight from the local airport
tourists over – I've flown one myself;
sometimes an airbase jet. Plane! Is it one of ours?
Together we watch it fly right over buildings and people.

Berwick Station at night

Only the old stopping train tells me
when to get up and open the door.
A young man follows, already
the giver of unwanted attention.
We sway together before the train finally halts.

The station's closed and empty
expecting only to be passed by.
The rain's hard and dark.
There's a small gate to a small car-park.
I walk like a boxer, like a dyke
until the man recedes into his own small car.

I wait for my lift, my back to the night.
A dog wind slobbers at my coat.
One station notched here on a rail;
one light on a chain of dimming lights
stretched right down to the sea.
Around dark houses sit with their own significance.
The sky doesn't change.
My own headlights take a long time coming.

The bridge loves the firth
For Grant

It is really a kind of sea space with clouds and gulls and shells

but it is not, in fact it is the buckled heart of the bridge:
its muscled stanchions wrapped in weed and tide
and frame braced for storm or calm feathers of salt.

Here the wind beats the wires above my head:
it is a humorous wind laughing out nine times
against the confines of the firth and its policy,
a kind of electricity – those taut cables;

a wind that plucks out music from the river
just the place where it becomes the sea and knits the fresh
and the salt. This is the spot you promise me
Dundee cake in a jute bag, a letter from McGonagall's doctor

and in return I'll backhand Selkie bannock, wrapped in a poem
tied up with a bramble.
                                    Space, the wind is laughing
but today is all knots and hasn'ts, even the gannets
stitching the water tight.

A chemical examination of Melrose Abbey

Friedländer's dyeing theory is tested by train excursion to Melrose
in search of lichen. Here it is said to grow in swags on trees
and even a preliminary stroll by the river Tweed
reveals interest. It may not be necessary to travel
to Northumberland after all.

He sits now warming by the fire. It is raining and somehow the wet
is dripping down into those draped trees. The air
and new-built villas in a clean-cut stone
a laboratory of colour
compared to the mill of smoke-filled town.

Nodding to the party of James Darling and sons
up from Suffolk though the father is a local man
he eavesdrops plans to go to Roxburgh or North.
The old haunts might be shown but they decide against.
There is no time. There never will be.

Friedländer steps out later in the damp to view the abbey
and its primitive tanning pits, the acidic conditions
undoubtedly achieved by the most intimate of chemicals.
The great nave itself is repaired and even at dusk and night
accepts an onslaught of visitors from the attached hostelry.

He recalls the poet Scott walked here alone by moonlight:
the cane and long length of him rimed in a spell-binding frost.
And to Friedländer's tired eyes, his ghostly shape and pattern remain.
But on closer examination of the walls and tracework,
the lichen exudations are all scraped away.

The tanning pits

Also used for dye, the colours available
dependent on season and lichen.
A job for the lay brothers
perhaps a promotion from the barn
and hot breath of living stock.
Tools arranged neatly once the skin
flung onto to a straw-covered floor
and the scraping begins.

Two boys for a large hide
one to hold, the older with the knife
close to these were tended more specialised pools
clouded with a stagnant tannic peat
the strips of putative leather
half rot proto shoe and belt
the stench of industrial urine
buckets of water sluicing the culvert
effluent splashing the tanner's careful
collection of cones and pine needles.

Dye works

12,000 murex shells that summer in Naples
to check Friedländer's chemical indigo
against royal purple. It did not match
its clotted blood. He made that too. And sold it.

Think about Capri and blues; that bit of sea
where Neapolitans cling together
in the boat's bottom, each rowing bench
as hard together as their own warm ribs.

And the cameos a slate-blue in paper boxes
on stalls amongst the Roman gravestones.
The puff of ochre smoke as couples stop
in the bothy of volcanic fumes for health.

Or lemons. Or watermelons selling to tourists.
Black sand and paid for royal blue deckchairs.
And skin as translucent as boys diving for pennies
the shine of water on them, holiday colour.

Industrial lichen

A room of a certain temperature,
the empty microscope bank
and much handled slides
engulfing equipment that pitches
almost to the plastic sheets
ghosting the wet area door.

The bio-hazard sign is peeling
and always ignored.
This was only ever about dye:
an array of washing up tubs
colour-coded
by a stained residue of dust.

Someone's jacket still hangs
next to the plastic bag marked "party".
Mould on the cloakroom wall
in dark red rings circled by orange.
The green ferns on the windowsill
flourish in the empty mill.

Leaving home

The rain bought out all the worms.
The pavement was wet with them

and snails. We had to tread carefully
although there were minutes left

until the train. The priority
your departure

to our unknown destination.
The reality avoided by a chain of oblique steps.

Frankenstein

The child in the womb
owns all its treasures. The animal
in the pipe that drowned
and stuck moulded to a new shape
by watery bloat;
the fur coat of a man
drops a new pelt.
We could make this into something:
if we could only scour
with salt and oatmeal;
arsenic makes it last.

How we could grow:
re-attaching amputations
and our eyes could gain eyes
see more.
That rock on the top
of the mountain: why
don't you step off and fly?

My son's ears were taut at birth,
an elfish right angle;
he needed to quit electric
but flitting meant a carthorse doctor
dragging him like a tree
from the acre wood
on the end of a chain.

All the snowdrops crushed
but look at the new sown garden;
new world. New man.

Today

a porridge of ice melts on Market Square
a day of returns and
the timely purchase of birthday cards
the post office queue

and the rain pelts down on railway station faces
nobody is crying
the diamond unmined is dark stone
and the rivers flow again

Knockturne
after David Blyth's installation inspired by cosmonaut Valentina
Tereshkova's return journey to Earth and the birth of his first child.

the machine of reproduction on a rinse cycle
all the little lambskins hung out to dry
on the antennae of my craft

I am here in a small room
with all my riches inside
sealed in a cubicle
                whirling in fluid

the knife cuts the cord between lamb and ewe
so cold its red breathed steam
and the long maternal tongue
                          licked into shape into life

is my space my mother
my child in utero
snuggle me in clean wool

my ship is drawn by still-born lambs
who hold the traces
take me home

The drove road

that long walk we took up the strath
the path expiring into turf and quartz

erratics and moraine clumped
the way led here and we followed

no beasts but us as we chewed our opposition
to each other in companionable strides

no dogs at our heels wheeling
at distractions

no turfy bothies unpeopled by us
children unmade migrated

that long walk we took up the strath
the empty land our only market

Missing the queimada

Arriving late, too smart for our own good
and for this party, the dregs
after the incantation
and the flames died down.
Chupitas served because we were invited
but without taste.

Our expat hostess, engaged to an absent
Colombian, bland in her peccadillos,
jewels and bottle lens;
all acquired here.
My navy suit was too small and too big
with the shadow of my better self.

Drunk driven by her sailing instructor
we rolled to the street of bars
for boiled eggs and razor fish.
It made us so sick in the morning
dissecting the flesh
our own lives never did ignite.

Tryst at the Ménagerie

A place for bad animals:
chimps with headaches,
a tiger tearing at its own tail.
Twining through the fag-ended
paths held in iron bars,
lovers discuss gifts and shopping.
"Do you want me to buy you things?"

A camel farts and shits lengthily
surrounded by neat Euro-children.
"No, my husband buys the presents."
The pair slide into the snake room.
Outside the Jardin des Plantes,
opaque windows twitch.

Another cold war

Bubble gum in the hotel salad
but the off-season stars look the same.
Wind from the south blows right in
rocking the Esperanza boats, stroking the hair
of the spliffed-up kids waiting,
as we suck the salt off our poorly-lit margaritas.

Sweating, once we cycle right round
the island to picnic alone at Green Beach
beyond the flag, fuel tank, and pre-fabs
that constitute headquarters.
Our passports unchecked, *"americanos"*.
We have already disappeared.

I find you swimming in suncream
reading a book about Russia.
I sit naked in the pool at night.
Tree frogs frame a composite of eighteen
identifiable sounds from palms,
flamboran, other plants, birds, the old hotel;
mangos bombing dark water.
Retrieving the fruit,
I put it on the poolside
for nobody to eat.

Yesterday in Esperanza,
we bought a coke from the shack.
Kahlo-like pictures transfix its flimsy walls.
Anonymous. Her face replaced by the island
in its many incarnations, bleeding,
cut by knives, slogan-ed, brandishing guns.
A contradictory smile remains.

The hairsheep

Let me write the story of sheep. I am the shepherd.
They sell at $2. Of course I sell them all
because a flock of sheep is the answer, because a flock of sheep
provides food, drink, clothing, company, text;
our rule over the sea of palimpsest.

The experiments of hide
as the skin, stretched and scraped in tannery urine,
takes the strigil's imprint. The original science of it
glimpsed by a blood-smoked labourer – it's good, will sell
at market – and years after its smeared birth sits
in a chained library unshifted. The loved one inside a high garden
stares out still to see a panting knight:
the forest, the sex, the bloody wounds.
Who could recognise in unwound parchment
the flickering messages that once clogged city drains?

    The sheep lies down with the pen *agnus stili*

Outside Gulu we're buying sheep to make into golf gloves: the skin
is so fine; the ratio of follicles allows a stretchability; forget calf.
Get my cell. I want my *Titleist* fingers! Swoosh my custom *Nikes*!

    It is estimated that around 10 percent of world sheep population is
    hairsheep

These odd non-sheep have little dollar signs above their heads.
I want to farm them but, too much trouble here, they stray:
they are the sheep on the edge, virtual, the marginalia of sheep.

    Let me write the story of sheep I am the shepherd

I roam the mountains and point my Zastava at wolves. I tell you
let's do business:

parchment – *parchemin* – the paper of Pergamum/Bergama
for sheep. And I'll score what I sang: my qawwalis, my sheep
babble, all my semantics. Until clean of sex, and even love,
only the signals that scrub and dust gave me remain; rock lizard path
ways and the ashes I used to write it down.

Words, today's algorithm, rising on a screen to stain the pelt
scraped by some slaughterman who understands a skin.
Once defiled, these scraps contain all the old libraries of the west.
Forget papyrus. Those sheep of the rough ground scratch a living,
sold to hold the hands of sportsmen grown fat on
manicured lawns in green fountain paradise (digits
houris might site) protected by the unmarked exploitable skin
of hairsheep. Odd electric sheep. On the signpost skin,

    there are no words.

Kestrel

a rise corner of red improbable on motorway berms
always at the edge of my eye behind scots pines
paling the vicarage garden

somehow a field skeined in lace a warm library
coded footsteps the now of it most important
the full strength colour
of twice-dyed plaid the place to hang
in the air and breathe in
nothing but the junction below
how long can hover be
how can hover
hover now can how the stoop talons
empty shrew-stopped
the bright trail recedes
as rodent micturate evaporates

this bird the lowest even a serf
could own its prey mice and shrew
no meal for any so all can eat
and hunt the hawk the lightest
six ounces of them
the falconer in gauntlet sits on the battered chair
until this raptor breaks and eats from the hand
neither can move until this eating
too long about it this little dies
his killer starved to hunt
too starved to hunt and kill
the falconer cannot shift them his elegant
commodity from a hunched last roost

sixty glimpses of grass to our twenty could you take
that empty room even a rabbit
what do you see below
what exudations? will you break me?

Digital age

A new relief is the search for perfect dirt
in computer films; all those smooth limbs
jeans, boob tubes and hairless faces
taut as a seventies' porn star. A programmer's

time spent with cylinders and cubes
engineering members and houses.
The soda and the baseball and the freebies
solidified into kids and pounds and pixels.

The accretion of texture:
hair on the lip of a virtual bank manager,
mud on the flagstone, blood stains and ripples,
a shagpile of yellow gorse on out-of-shot hills.

Thinking about Embla outside Edinburgh

A tunnel of trees scuttled by leaves like withered rats
the last to leave and bound by work
that journey again split from Pathhead
on a slick of grey water the rain gouts down
panicking my wipers

eventually on the by-pass the light gloams
and water deepening the car takes off
an uneasy moment when the ground's not there
I enter the stream and wish I could float

away to a Valckenborch spring and a landing
between the bloody lists and may gathering
dewy possibilities of the green walk
instead distracted by sandbank oystercatcher prints,
an ember in a labyrinth, I drift up on Easter Road.

The mews house

The door at the back is the one I prefer.
Its viscous handle still damp at midday
sited where no breeze can dry or use.
A green skin shines uneven bricks.

Chewing the air, I've forgotten the bright sun
of the front square, its carriage-able sweep,
tight-gated garden all breasted with bloom
like a girl in a balcony bra. I don't want

an easy ride. I want your thin blankets.
The back bedroom's lack of light so thick
I cannot write a word
unless I look hard. Unless, my love, I think.

Walking the lime tree drive that time
with the sky all swinging blue
around our fingers and you
masquerading as the wealthy industrialist
all this is mine. I almost believed
you would give it up for me.

Or we're older and I'm back in town
with you attentive in a softly-carpeted hall.
This time I imagine a government job:
a desirable unobtrusive place.

Later I suppose we might go out
not overdressed
to a dinner slightly spoiled
by respective middle-aged appetites

but for now our eyes meet
before you take my coat or scarf
and comment on country weather.
The mirror is gold and quiet.

Border snow

the noise is not the noise of the street
but of the hill filtered through snow
I imagine that this is the start of a cave
its birth a river's fingertip

becoming sink hole until I and all my friends
if I had them with me would be sunk
in a cavern, Merlin might be there
cooking something warm

because beneath the hill is the core of the hill
and that is cold
cold enough to hurt your brain
and make you think of them again

I might put on the old armour
and the wizard would be glad measuring time
in his saucepan and chocolate
we would discuss the newspaper

oh yes, he has them very old and webby
like granddad's shelf lining in the shed
he needs to keep in touch
so he sings some snippets of song and makes

a rude gesture that is actually unknown to me
and that breaks the ice
the river flows right through depositing me
here by somebody's Volvo

Angel

Blake's angels sat in the tree
spitting down visions. Mine
malinger in street corners
checking their pulses.

Have you seen the square
solid old men perambulating?
Well, just lift up the corner
of their drab macs and

do you see the neon?
Do you see the brightest –
the highest drop – beneath?
They are paradise nudgers

and painful deaths reconciled
in the cut of a felt homburg.
Their faces, ugly as sin,
remind me to wash regularly.

*

ANGELS – they're not at all fat –
fleshy but solid like my Dad.

Their hands warmed mine once. I
used to feel their breaths on me.

Further examination showed plaster
feathers make hard wings the most

striking feature of their earth
uniform and… shit, the offensive
smell proves how human are – ANGELS

The bomb cats

I glimpsed their absences around the pigsty:
an eye, a tooth, leg gone on one, kinked
useless tail uncurling. Then a mean magpied face
scrunched in recoil still from that blast.

My grandmother spoke of the blanket
from Belfast that wrapped them;
so everyday, so dirty. They were lucky.
And I wanted their certainty

raking the minute organs they left,
perfect and unreclaimable, for signs.
They disappear haunting a forgotten space,
as would all the casual killers that I hunted.

A walk around Preston Island

Reclaimed ash, yet it's all water sound, culverts
and curlews, a shelduck glimpse with wing tucked,
as we nose around for sloes and hawthorn bread
and cheese. The salt was made here

for three hundred years before the firedamp blast.
The pan remains by a stealthy wharf:
four men and one woman tending the broth,
inconstant land distilled to cash.

Here because webby shafts could be shovel scrabbled
for the stub coal to fire both sea salt and whisky.
Was it the wrong smoke? or lack of stoke
stopped it? But you can trawl beaches for littoral coal,

rowboat an underwater mine now pattern of reed-wisp.
Lagoons built within soot spit floated from Longannet;
its skeleton still in the distance receding
decommissioned bones all plucked.

A trickling current echoes in the scrubby bushes
with the migrant birds blown in and tight
to spindly branches created and attacked with industry
plucking fruit with spirit.

Firing range

Taking aim at the small targets:
baked pigeons that fly over the overgrown turf.
This is practice but then it was war.

My feet slip into the rabbit holes,
butterflies and beyond only the firth and no sign
of the full samandar

we used to pound the strand
recoiling imagined one-time warship thud on dummy trains –
analysis of distance, statistical accuracy –

always behind you hunting tracks, bullets.
You knew what to shoot for: the metal shell
casings all salt-pitted as if a sea-transported fruit, blackberries.

In fact, it looked like nothing unnatural. Sometimes we
mould into your soldiers in camouflage,
fired up in the dug-outs on the edge of the marram range.

But it is all over; out-of-date even when you
trained by yourself in these hills with a small dog
just running round until

jungle summit sniped religiously, yelling at
the sous-lieutenant ils se trouvent derrière
l'arbre but uncovering the word *darakht*
darakht you never forgot again

at night always on exercise; fighting back to soft mist and cadets
or a final shooting gallery pentland climb down into
our shattering family kiln; ghosts of crazed
flags laid low on quartz.

In my pocket the beach bramble stone dunts in a box.
I have no better word for it today:
no ricochet spark strikes out your name
only the choice of this cold line of clay.

What you were left with

The pith of the house was what you were left with
the sun inching day by day along the wall
and the manor and the fig tree
from your chair you could count the days
of winter by red brick measurements
note them down in a number of books

The structure of your desk was what you were left with
notebooks and blotter and intray aligned
the animal pencil and pen set with the double lid
the fox strolled precise from one to the other
nothing went out accounts stopped
the sun on the red wall

The red chair and its stool was what you were left with
coaster and control and ashtray tobacco
that wouldn't tamp and nurses
and your left ankle that couldn't rest
on the red footstool
the sun going down as you predicted

Collecting seaweed

Sweet bather nestling but not now as chafe legs
walk further into the salt

no fun no capers rubber gloves
that shred at the fingertips

and only the right type sorted underwater
damp library cards

sometimes mask on I look at the silver jelly rocks
underwater and my hair escaping beanie prison

reaches out weightless
the crimpy soft folds of endless plush

grandmother's settee loose coverings
and tide push and loop

the expensive stuff out of reach
on the sand I am in my element again

so why does the salt on my skin pinch me
ephemeral weather

business drips
dillybag drying to nothing at my hip.

Doggerland harvest

We are exploring forgotten seafloor
geography as the plane slips into Schiphol.
My masked neighbour, ex-navy surveyor,
navigates bombscape drilled into Neolithic

for windfarms using a digital weather-eye,
submersible and deep dives to rub sludge
and crop bombs; factory fresh, as he puts it,
if they are German or in state of decay.

The uncertain degrading is the biggest risk:
volatile shares on the shoal path in mounds
that might have been furrow, midden, eggshell,
antler in the missing oak tree.

At the sea clearing where once grain was cut and soon
mills will farm the air again; it's
a simple matter of locating unspent explosions.
Were we at the academy together?

Did we walk the landbridge
pathed with acorns, the farmstead,
fertile land that joins us?
And we are once again raked by seed and promise.

A rhetorical question just like where and when
does Europe end. Maybe later
without quarantine or delay an unlikely yield
threshing together in that lost shortcut.

Auto-immunity
For Pru

Horror autotoxicus: the failure of self
to know itself
fighting self's tissues and cells.

Ehrlich predicted this, before Frankfurt,
the cigar box
and the rabbit saved from syphilis.

Animal tissue scraped and stained
in careful rank:
dye perhaps a magic bullet to root out ill.

Its colour at first mistaken
for healing
but health still occurred.

And Ehrlich's legacy, the street with his name?
Stained in war, torn down,
but lights camera! flesh and blood restore.

Old Biddy

My son never comes to see his dear old mum.
Calls me that on the phone. Of course,
it whispers like the neighbours,
that house is too big for her.
Too small when him and the others were kids.
They've all gone now:
dropped me like petals drop a flower.

And look at the garden, they whisper behind
my bindweed-covered wall. It's wild, a disgrace.
She'll fall. Break her hip. We'd never know.
They'd know and like it:
they always watch me garden, whispering,
out at all hours. Picking. poking. planting.
It's my garden, isn't it? He'd like me to stop
by the window waiting for visiting hours.
Well, the only time I've ever seen him walk up
that street with a smile, he thought I'd died.

I wouldn't answer the phone. Why should I?
It's my house not his. Not Jack's.
And the phone whispers, leave it.
It's my garden too. I bend, like a big tree
wind-lurching, to keep it. But I'm sharp enough
to let apple- and horse-mint, budge out the weeds.

I use maybe five leaves a year:
so they grow and grow. Rosemary's so little,
I take her up in for winter. Sniff her spikes
for comfort. Coltsfoot and hyssop soothe coughs,
but not for her. She's more vulnerable to cold
than I am. Lavender caresses my sleep breath,
but I'll never need raspberry leaves for pains
and sickly pregnancy. The canes are broken.

Lemon balm infused with elderflower sweetens kisses.
Jack wondered about pennyroyal for cramps.
Why do you cramp? Why? He cramped me,
my womb squeezed me like his tight ways.
Sex was so "dirty", he'd never clean his piddler
and I'd sit up half the night in juniper baths
restoring my special place – that he never touched
I mean, put a hand to, never licked or saw.

All those worried women at Glaze the chemist's
where I once worked: what if I'd told them
about blood-pain and cures, instead of pills
for feminine conditions? Or better, don't kill the pain,
use it! To goad your self into leaving, action
then soak in sleepy geranium water, and think
about being a woman
instead of cutting it away like your toenails.

They'd think I meant sex. The huge
unmentionable. Well, whatever, I was too young
at first to be telling them, then too old.
The space behind the counter was too small
for women to be friendly. I'll never fall over
in my garden though. I'm old, not bonkers:
if it's wet, I don't go out, a wet garden all tangled.
Sometimes if it's dark, I'll step outside the backdoor
unseen and listen to the soft nothing like water.

I'm not often frightened but I don't cook hardly now,
my wrists slow-knobbled. The kitchen smells, of course.
I leave pans on the stove: can't lift the weight.
Been carrying those two heavy men too long.
Garden makes me think of Mother. She showed me how.
That's what I remember. Meaning. I remember Jack
like a rain shower, no, I'm touched by rain.
Jack was necessity. Sharing? I told him nothing.
It was our way. And my girls: well, Jack named them.
They write. I'm not blameless.

I didn't want to be left with one.
I remember the little lad, now lying.
Dear old mum, he whispers, sell the house.
It'd be his big break. To make me wait
to watch him coming through a box window,
like he's on telly. But now he has to wait for me
like a sick child to vomit.
And my chamomile's dead – frozen in
that last cold snap before the spring.

Saltmarsh

what is here? what is missing? on the shoreline a woman
plods oystercatchers into flight

the mud grips grass here until land forms
not one thing or another these pools where print runes

tell of feeding, the sand probe bills
and even more wormcasts left behind as tide recedes

and the dredge of sand fragments of shell is
pulled, no marimba

just a cold longshore pitted with goosander pixels
a smirr of ducks the walker lost to flight

French room *

It is all about hats. How pretty they can make you.
She sleeps under the arbour of honeysuckle and roses.
For a spell, she works you into a space of embroidery.

Planned to help the sale of high-priced hats in a number of ways.
They create an atmosphere of exclusiveness and distinction.

We might sit in Woolf's room. The room of her own.
No one else can sit here with us.
The maid brings in tea and toast.
Virginia likes to eat in
a workmanlike way but crumbs fall
likes stones into her pockets.
Never quite good enough is it?

The quiet seclusion gives the salesperson an advantage,
as well as implying a special attention to the customer.

The girl brushes titbits from the sill into the garden
tumbling for the wren not the robin.
Marie-Antoinette ties them into her pigtails
and then so does everyone else.

Salesrooms of this nature are richly furnished and
generally decorated in light colours, affording a more
delicate background for the exquisite hats shown in them.

A golden shoe. It does not fit.
Its heel will break.
I still want it.

Since it is desirable to give every advantage to customers
and salespeople in the disposal of high-priced merchandise,

the "special" rooms usually have daylight for
selecting and matching colours.

The beauty therapist's gone next door.
I relax as instructed
while acid eats my lashes.
I can't see myself.

Dark French rooms are sometimes very effective.
Customers have said that in such rooms any hat looks becoming.

That girl is to blame for fetching fuel after dark.
He schools her mechanically against the splintering kindling.
She sleeps under the arbour of honeysuckle and roses.

For a spell, she works you into a space of embroidery.
It's all about hats isn't it? If I tell you a pretty story –
I can stay alive as long as you like.

A number of small separate rooms designed to separate [the robin
from the wren]: these rooms are quite often distinguished
by some special name, such as the "French Room."

* *All italic quotes found in* Millinery *by*
Charlotte Rankin Aiken, B.A. (1922)

The darning flat

They work hard-nosed like hacks or architects on under-lit desks
technical drawing
they seek a clue, the missing pipe, the cable or high-tension
beam in a tartan
almost need a chisel to mend

wrapped in fashion cloth waterfalling, the three women hunt
the head ends for a lost thread
this takes a pool of silence, touch, training
a year and a half at college
above all an eye and taste for it

sometimes the break is caught at the stuttering loom
the operator winding back the spindles – his unheard sigh –
and ties a knot. sometimes sixty yards are flawed.
that's all.
the flat women, pin back their ears, needle, yarn, make whole.

Climbing above Kinlochleven

Forget forecasts. Let's aim up,
ignorant. The small grey town,
wedged into Loch Leven,
drops like blood to the heart.

Grabbing a pinch of blue sky,
we climb into Na Gruagaichean
Up here, the loch becomes sea,
the path ice. And a few flakes come.

Spare socks for gloves, and the snow
sweeps us up. Like monkeys, we run
for the lee, where lazy whorls push damp
white into sandwiches and faces.

Rock beneath our waterproofs
beats against yours and mine.
Warm limbs. Snow falls. Wait.
Is there a way down?

Investigating, blanketed steps
until the sky is ours again.
Dive into the circulation of the valley.
We are the road home.

The trouble with lichen

1. *With Beatrix at Dalguise*

Aurora and her books down by the burn
she stares at rock
volumes tumbled in her lap
a piece of heather in her hair
sketched like that by Landseer

but the girls are looking at lichen
cross-referencing its open cups
a stone university
later in the study they take out the microscope
stealthily before crumpets

2. *Marianne*

the flowerpots started it; the search
for what? first to cleanse, why
were they always dirty? crusting
with time and absence
such hazy frondage I wouldn't
have eaten the contents of their shadowed cups
saucers and vases
now in the laboratory I take them
to pieces their fruiting parts
I have to know
I look at the white wall tufted with horse hair
and wonder.

3. *Germination of the spores of the Agaricineae*

another letter from Beatrix full of ferns
and fungus; her paper heart
encased in a male body,
mysteries next to little pictures of
dressed up rabbits
work passed off as belonging to others
spore wants bacteria
men who sail away and leave us
to investigate and write
capillaries strained to classification
I order 200 hundred trees from France
and tell her the varieties.

So here we go again

at the side of the garage the one with the red fascia shining
but a kind of dial place we remember only

because it reminds us of something else
your colour your buttons your hands
none of them are close to me

but the garage was a sign install brighter
neither once was somehow that the comfort
when I follow behind becoming smaller

and smaller sold clicking numbers with a chocolate bar
stolen in my hand and melting

Rain was red at the end

Pattering on people's shoulders like a promise kept
and then starting arguments and off the leaves
that reached for it but instead fell themselves
in shards and drifts tiding the pavement edge.

And we laughed and ate pistachio ice cream
sharing tips on wrapping and ribbons
while those on the edge washed away in the red
water much thicker than the blood that binds us.

Notes

The poem 'Cowboys and cowgirls' is taken from the film screenplay *Rachel and the Stranger*, 1948. Directed by Norman Foster. With Loretta Young, William Holden, Robert Mitchum. The plot is slightly adapted.

The found sections in the poem 'French rooms' are taken from *Millinery* by Charlotte Rankin Aiken, B.A. 1922.

'Queimada' has Galician Celtic origins and the spell spoken during its preparation confers special powers on its drinkers.

The title of the poem sequence 'The trouble with lichen' is borrowed from the 1960 science-fiction novella by John Wyndham.

Henry Schunck was a Manchester chemist of German origin who is known for his innovative work on dyes. Paul Friedländer was a German dye chemist who also worked on indigo substitutes. Although he is likely to have known Schunck's work on indigo their meeting here is imaginary. Schunck's lab is set up in the Manchester Museum of Science and Industry. Paul Ehrlich was a German physician who invented an early technique using dye on tissues to identify cells. He also discovered a cure for syphilis. The street named after him in Frankfurt was removed during the Nazi regime because of his Jewish faith but information including a film starring Edward G Robinson in 1941 (*Dr Ehrlich's Magic Bullet*) made him hard to overlook. Post-war, the street name was restored.

Thanks to:

—Professor Robert Christie and Dr Britta Kalkreuter of Heriot-Watt University for answering my questions on dye chemistry.

—Lochcarron Selkirk for allowing me access to Waverley Mill darning flat.

—Louise Jury for reblurbing my blurb with great patience.

—Rip Bulkeley for pointing out that I only wrote in black and white.